T0208682

DESTROY THIS
DEVO

A 35 Day Devotional for Kids

ANDY BROWN

WESTBOW
PRESS®
A DIVISION OF THOMAS NELSON
& ZONDERVAN

WestBow Press books may be ordered through booksellers or by contacting:

WestBow Press
A Division of Thomas Nelson & Zondervan
1663 Liberty Drive
Bloomington, IN 47403
www.westbowpress.com
1 (866) 928-1240

ISBN: 978-1-9736-4922-9 (sc)
ISBN: 978-1-9736-4921-2 (e)

Library of Congress Control Number: 2018914959

Print information available on the last page.

WestBow Press rev. date: 02/06/2019

This book is being destroyed by

_____

Things I love to eat

_____

Favorite games to play

_____

If I had $517.38 I would buy

_____

I love Jesus because

_____

If you find this book, please return it to
the person who looks like this:

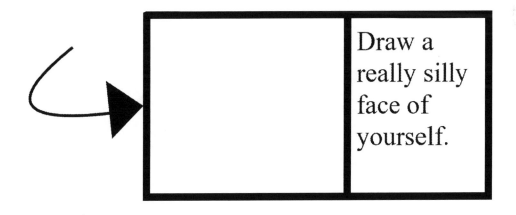

Draw a really silly face of yourself.

What exactly is Destroy This Devo?

One of my favorite Bible verses is Mark 10:15: "Truly I tell you if anyone does not receive the Kingdom like a child, they will never enter it. (NIV)" This passage got me thinking "How do children like to learn." and "What can be done to help kids want to read the Bible more?" After teaching for 8 years in elementary school and working in children's ministry for over 10, I learned a few things that helped me answer these questions. *Destroy This Devo* is a children's devotional that kids can use to grow a personal relationship with God. But not in your conventional way.

It is my prayer that through the use of this new kind of devotional, children will actually *want* to read and use the Word of God. This book is a hands-on approach which can create instant memories of what God is doing in their lives. It is also my prayer that the Bible verses used in *Destroy This Devo* will increase their scripture memory, with the help of their parents or caregivers. By reading the given passages and using them in tangible ways, children can create a strong suit of armor (Ephesians 6:11) while wreaking havoc on the book.

How to Use This Book

There are thirty-five individual devotionals in *Destroy This Devo*. Each one pertains to either a life application in general or to children's lives more directly. However, each devotional is intended to draw readers to a personal relationship with Jesus at the center of it all.

Children should only complete one activity a day rather than go through the whole book in a few sittings. If they work through one devotional activity a day, they can easily soak in the passage and the meaning behind it all. If they race through the text, the effectiveness could be lost, and the book might seem more like a toy than a learning tool.

Since parents are the greatest teaching tool a child has for shaping their lives in Christ, parental participation is strongly suggested. Parents who work with their child can also learn more, just as Isiah 55:11 says: "So My word that goes out of My mouth: It will not return to me empty, but accomplish what I desire and achieve the purpose for which I sent it."

Destroy This Devo is designed to be 100% hands-on. I want children to want to use the book. Creative expression is a teaching technique professional educators and presenters use to fit the many learning styles they see in their classrooms. Through my experience as a children's pastor and school teacher, I have learned how to reach a diverse group of children with lasting lessons using seriously crazy lessons.

Lastly, children are to memorize as many scripture verses as possible. A reward system that parents and children come up with together can help with this. The devotionals are not in chronological order, so your family is free to choose which devotional they want to complete each day. If the family is missing supplies to finish the hands-on portion of the devotional, there should be no stress about completing it; the supplies can be gathered for a later time.

My prayer is that through this book, your family has fun working through the pages together, grows closer to each other, and experience a life change through Christ.

Ok, so let's review what you're supposed to do with *Destroy This Devo:*

1) Complete one devotional a day (in any order you choose)
2) Work together with your family
3) Memorize as many Scripture verses and stories possible
4) Don't take it easy on this book!
5) Have fun destroying!

The Bible says we should all have the faith of a mustard seed. Why a mustard seed? Because it is one of the smallest seeds in the world that turns into a monster size tree. This doesn't mean we should have a tiny faith, but that even the smallest faith in our Lord can do huge things. Read Matthew 17:20-21 and talk about what this means. How much you do trust in God? How big do you want your faith to grow?

Finger paint a mountain with real mustard (or with anything yellow) on this page and pray God will help grow your faith.

One night during a terrible storm, Jesus walked out on the water to meet his disciples who were having a terrible time in the boat. When Peter saw Jesus, He called Peter out of the boat. Good old Peter stepped out in courage but starts to sink when he takes his eyes off of Jesus. Jesus saved Peter immediately but think about the courage Peter had to have to step out of the boat. Are there times you lack the courage to do something awesome? Pray that God will help you be courageous to face the storms in your life.

Read Matthew 14:22-32. Color in and cut out the image of Peter and pretend to have him stand and walk on water. Let him dance, do back flips, and whatever else you can think of. Remember to make sure to save him just like how Jesus saved Peter when he starts to sink.

The Bible says we must fight the good fight. No, really it does. Maybe not the fighting you see in an ultra cool ninja movie, but the battles we have everytime the world tries to lead us off God's path.

Read 1Timothy 6:12 and then ready your heart by ninja chopping this book 10 times (or even more if you want) while yelling "Fight the good fight of faith!" like a ninja.

Something that will help you go far in life is knowing what God's plans are for you. We have to be careful that we are not chasing a plan that God has made for someone else. Their success might not necessarily be what God has in store for you. What does God want YOU to do? Do you know what it is? Have you prayed about it? Read Ecclesiastes 4:4 and Ephesians 5:15-17. Then, spend time in prayer to help you know clearly what His plans are for you.

Now grab some bubble juice or make a homemade solution of dish soap and water, grab a bubble wand (or make one), and have someone blow bubbles in the air. Try catching as many bubbles on these pages as you can. For every bubble you catch, tell God thank you for His plans for your life.

Let's play a little game. Have someone put a blindfold on you and lead you around the house without touching you. Listen for their voice so you don't run into anything. Try to get into every room. You can even try to make your favorite lunch like a PB&J while someone is watching you (just so you don't get hurt). What else can you try while the blindfold is on?

- Feed your pet?
- Mop the floor?
- Clean up your room?

Ok ok, now take the your blindfold off and read ahead.

2 Corinthians 5:7 says:

"We live by faith and not by sight" (NIV)

Talk about what it was like to walk around not being able to see where you were going or even what you were doing. Our faith in Jesus has to be just that, FAITH. Sometimes we trust too much in ourselves and not enough in God. Pray that God will help you grow your faith in Him.

God's Word, the Bible, is said to be sweeter than anything else. Not that we can literally eat the Bible mixed in a bowl of icecream and expect a blast of sugary goodness, but rather God's Word is good for our soul. It keeps us close to Him where we belong. What is best for our eternity is perfect for us now. Read Psalms 119:103. After you do, glue some of your favorite candy wrappers on the blank page over there to know how sweet God's Word really is. You can add more candy wrappers to the page as often as you want.

Not going to lie. Today's devo will be tough. God wants us to be kind to others. Even kind to those who are difficult to be kind to. Read Ephesians 4:32 and think about one person you need to be kind to while you read it. The person could be a sibling, a neighbor, a teammate. Anyone who might make you cringe a little when you think about them. Pray for that person, then write a kind letter on the next page to them, tear it out and hand it to them. Make sure to pray over it too.

Walking with integrity is important in our daily lives. Wait, what's that? You're not sure what the word integrity means? Well simply put, integrity is our attitude about how good and honest we are even when people are not watching you. If our level of integrity is high, we will choose to not lie and be nicer to people. This is more honoring to God and ourselves. Take a moment to read Proverbs 10:9 and hear what the Bible says about integrity.

Now that you better understand the word "integrity" lets put it into action.

Throw this book across the room (just make sure not to hit anything). While you are walking over to pick it up, pray out loud for God's help to stay pure and keep a strong integrity in yourself. Do this 4 or 5 times.

Lying

Cheating

Stealing

Jealousy

BAD WORDS

Let's be honest. The devil wants nothing more than to destroy your life. His plan is to make you believe that sin isn't that bad, but it is. We should target living our lives in Jesus to stop the devil's plans. Read John 10:10 in your Bible and talk about what the devil might be lying to you about right now. Then put this book on the ground and stand over it. Drop a sharpened pencil or marker from the height of your forehead and try to hit the sin words on the previous page. Keep going until you knock them all out. Race a partner to see who can do it the fastest.

Living in fear can sometimes feel like your in a jail cell. Just stuck there wanting to be freed of your fear but not able break out. We all have things that scare us: animals, sickness, loneliness. But fear can grip you and leave you struggling to find peace. God loves you so much He wants to free you from your fears. You simply need to choose to walk with Him and trust in His grace. It might sound too easy to just say we trust in God.

To help you out, read Psalms 23:4 in your Bible. Then think about what fears you have in your life, write them below, cut out the bottom half of this page (make sure to not cut out the wording on the next page), tear it into super small pieces, and pray for God to give you the strength to overcome your fears like a boss.

_____

_____

_____

_____

_____

_____

_____

_____

_____

_____

Ok, are you ready for a super easy concept that a lot of adults make complicated? Say the next line out loud:

"God created the world!"

It's true. How did He do it? Take a few minutes and read all of Genesis 1 with someone.

Write a list of the order of the 7 days on the space below.

Now for the really fun part. God created the universe from nothing. Let's see how you can do with something unexpected. Go to a trash can in your house and make some sort of art project out of what you find. Draw a picture of it here or glue it on this page. Just make sure to wash your hands when you're done.

Do you have someone in your life you just have a terrible time getting along with? A family member? The school bully? When someone hurts you emotionally or physically, we need to be careful how we react to them. Matthew 18:15 offers good advice on this subject. Read it over, and think about one person who has hurt you in some way. Pray for that individual. Then use the next page to journal how you think God wants you to start repairing the problem. Make sure you talk to you parent or another adult before you act on it.

THE MY BIG PROBLEM
PERSON PAGE

How does God want to use you to help heal the situation?

_____

_____

_____

_____

_____

_____

_____

_____

_____

Have you heard about this man named King Solomon? This young guy was crazy awesome! God wanted to bless his life so He said he would give him any ONE thing he asked for. He could of had ANYTHING. What he asked for was super cool! Read about King Solomon's experience with God in 1Kings 3:4-15, then cut out the prayer on the next page, decorate it however you want with whatever you want, and stick it up somewhere that you will see it and repeat it every morning for at least a week or more.

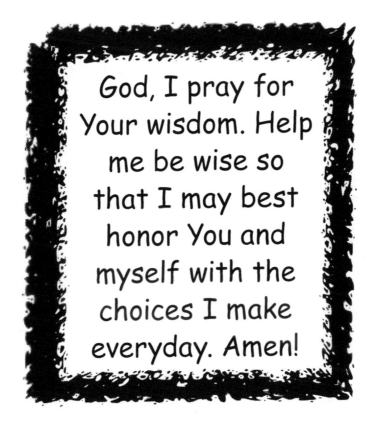

God, I pray for Your wisdom. Help me be wise so that I may best honor You and myself with the choices I make everyday. Amen!

Memorizing Scripture is a weapon we can use to beat up on the devil. It becomes an even better weapon when we teach others and have more people memorize it. Teach the Bible passage below to someone with hand motions you come up with and have them work to have it memorized for at least 5 days. You should give them a surprise pop quiz every once in a while to keep them sharp.

"So whether you eat or drink or whatever you do, do it all for the glory of God." 1 Corinthians 10:31 NIV

Jesus showed others how much He loved them by serving them. He didn't think "I'm the Son of God. You all need to serve Me." Instead, Jesus showed his love one night by washing the feet of his disciples before eating. He wants us to live our lives following His example and work to serve others in love. Even if it means we do things which may seem less than awesome. To God, this kind of life truly is AWESOME!!!!!

Take a moment and read John 13:1-17 with someone from your Bible. Talk about what it means to serve others and why it pleases God when we do that. Then go outside and make super messy mud puddle. Have you and someone else jump in it. Get your feet super messy. Step on the book and leave your footprints on these pages. Then wash their feet while you tell them how much you appreciate them and how much God loves them. Feel free to reverse the roles.

The story of Esther in the Bible is fantastic! It describes how a woman who was super scared of what God had called her to do, but in faith, overcame her fears with His help. She actually won the battle. Pick up your Bible and read the brave conversation she had with her uncle Mordecai in Esther 4:12-17. Talk out loud about how God can help you overcome your greatest fears. Then cut out the monsters on the next page and glue them to some random items. Set them up and use this book as if it were a real sword to knock them over like a warrior of God. Do that a few times using your best battle cry giving Him the glory.

39

The Book of Romans is full of imagery that reveals what God's love is truly like. There are so many things that happen in our lives that we don't deserve.

Mostly our salvation when we choose to receive Jesus in our hearts. To better understand this free gift, read Romans 6:22-23 and discuss what this gift of life from God means for us.

Afterwards, make a gift from your own hands that you can give to someone else. Write a note or just tell them "Here's a gift I want to give you for free because I care about you."

The best way to be ready for something is to have what you need already with you. This rule applies to being ready to fight the troubles we have in this world. So where should we put God's Word? The Bible tells us to hide His Word in our hearts. What do you think it means to hide the Bible in your heart? It means that we should read our Bibles daily not just to say we are reading it, but so that we can grow in it. Read how hiding God's Word in our heart was described about beautifully in Psalms 119:9-16.

Now chew a piece of gum for about 15 minutes (or until the flavor is gone). While you are chewing, pray to God to help you best hide His Word in your heart. Pray for as long as you are chewing. When you are ready, put your gum right here in the box and fold this page over it to hide your sugary treat.

When you see this page, remember how wonderful it is to have the Bible hidden in your heart.

"Whatever you do, work at it
with all your heart, as working
for the Lord, not for men"
Colossians 3:23

What would your life look like if you did everything like you were actually doing it with God right in front at you? I mean if you could literally see Him watching you? You would probably do it the best of your ability. We need to live our life like that in everything we do.

Read Colossians 3:23 on the previous page a few times. Then toss your devo in the air higher and higher each time saying "With all my heart, I will work for the Lord." Try to break your own height record.

There is an illustration called the Roman's Road that is used to help lead people who don't have Christ in their heart to begin a new life with Jesus. Its actually a very simple idea that looks like the one below.

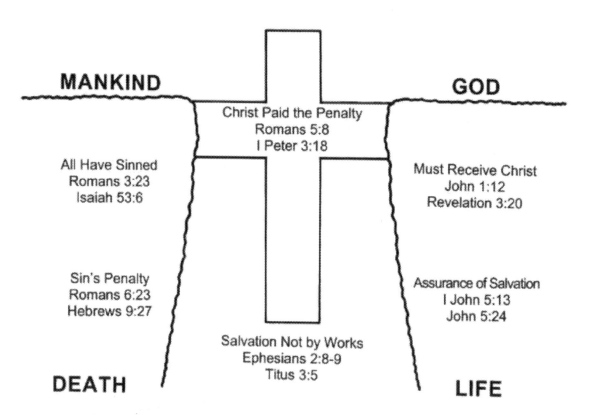

MANKIND

GOD

Christ Paid the Penalty
Romans 5:8
I Peter 3:18

All Have Sinned
Romans 3:23
Isaiah 53:6

Must Receive Christ
John 1:12
Revelation 3:20

Sin's Penalty
Romans 6:23
Hebrews 9:27

Assurance of Salvation
I John 5:13
John 5:24

Salvation Not by Works
Ephesians 2:8-9
Titus 3:5

DEATH

LIFE

Now here's a question for you:

"Where do you want to see yourself on that picture?" Hopefully you answered on the side of God. But how do we make sure we end up on the side with God? Read Romans 10:9-10 and choose one of the two choices from below

1. Pray for the first time asking Jesus to come into your heart.
2. Give thanks that you have prayed for Jesus to come into your heart and believe He living there right now.

Whichever you chose, make sure to share your answer with someone outside of your family. Color in the Roman's Road when you are done.

Have you ever wondered what God created us to be? Everyone has at one time or another. What we have to remember is that God does not create "accidents". His plan for you is exactly what He wants from you. Paul, who started out as a really bad dude, wrote the Book of Corinthians and said it best when he talked about how he doesn't deserve to be known as someone special. But God did call him to a huge world changing experience like no one could have ever expected.

Me Today	Future Me

Read 1 Corinthians 15:9-11 then draw a picture above of what you look like right now and what you think you will look like in the future with God's design in mind. Don't forget to pray for God's direction.

On a fruit tree, there will always be good fruit and bad fruit. God says the same thing about people. There will be people you find in life who look like something wonderful but in reality are nothing but bad fruit. We need to be careful not to be fooled by them by recognizing what they are in Christ. Think about the friends you hang out with the most at school or other places. Do you think how they act is something that is good and pleasing to God? Or do you think these friends are really going to get you in trouble?

You always need to be careful of those you are with because the devil will do everything he can to mess you up. Jesus tells us how we can best be ready to avoid bad fruit in Matthew 7:15-20. Read this passage then grab some fruit like an orange or an apple, stand this book up, and throw the fruit at it. Every time you hit the book, say one way you can recognize someone who makes bad fruit and someone who produces good fruit. When you are done, make a fruit salad with your projectiles. You may want to clean them up a bit first.

Think about this question. How much do you love money? The bad news is some people love money so much they can't let it go to be used for what God wants us to use it for. The Bible is very clear about how we are supposed to use money. Malachi 3:10 instructs us to make sure we don't forget that money is both a tool to help people and a tangible way God can bless. Read this out loud and say a prayer asking God for help in using money correctly in your life. Now grab a bunch of coins and challenge someone to see who can get the highest score flipping coins on the targets. When you are done, put all the money you used in a baggie and give it to your church in their next offering.

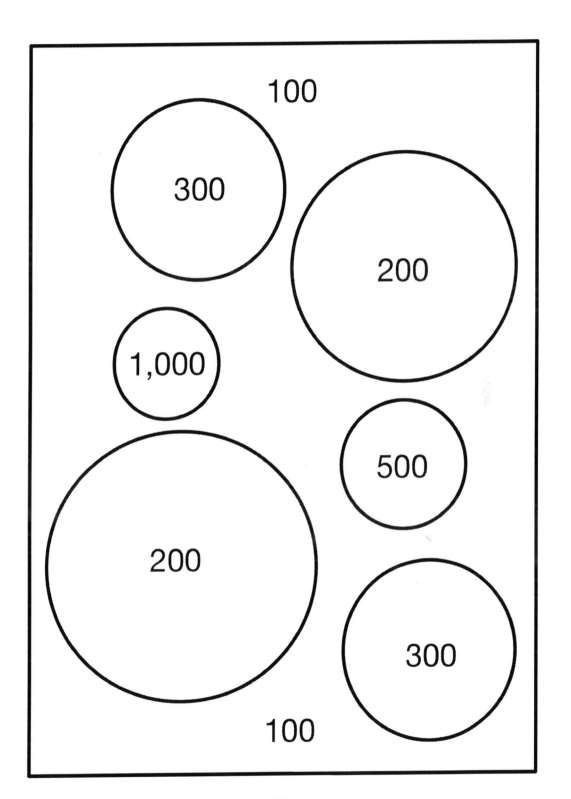

There is one distraction that brings even the most determined person to a screeching halt. That one thing is worrying. People that worry too much, think less about how much God is in control and more about the dreaded "What if?" question. When there is a huge problem that you can't see an answer to, stop and ask the One who has all the answers. God knows what is best for you and He loves you so much.

Take a few minutes and read Matthew 6:25-34. Talk with someone about what you worry about. Together, pray that God will ease your heart and mind about these things. Afterwards, go outside, gather some grass, wildflowers, dirt, and small rocks and make a garden scene on these 2 pages by gluing these items below. Use it to remember why we shouldn't worry but instead trust in God who loves you more than anything.

Do you like to sing? If you do (or even if you shy away from it), you should know this:

"GOD LOVES IT WHEN YOU SING PRAISES TO HIM!"

I mean he really loves it! Our songs of praise to God can actually bring joy back to you. There are times when sadness comes into our lives but when that happens, remember how much God loves you! He is absolutely crazy for you! When a guy named David was running for his life from a King who wanted to find him and end him, he began writing poems of joy and thanksgiving. It sounds bizarre that someone would find their cool in a terrible situation like this, but David knew who was in control.

This kind of thinking helped him write a whole lot of great stuff that actually ended up in the Bible. Read Psalm 100:1-5 to hear a super song of joy that will bring a smile to your face. When you're done reading that passage, role up this book like a microphone and pretend your a music star on stage. Sing your favorite songs of praise to God. If you don't know one, make a song up or just read Psalm 100 as if you are singing it out loud. Don't be embarrassed if you have an audience. You might even ask them to sing along with you to help you out.

The greatest gift we have ever been given is the gift of life forever in Heaven through the death and resurrection of Jesus Christ. It was all done according to the amazing plan God put into place. He knew that on our own, people would be lost and unable to live a sin-free life. But praise God, He sent His only son Jesus to earth to save all who call on Him. Not even death could keep Jesus buried. His sacrifice for us, is the greatest gift we can ever have. To help you remember this, read 1Corinthians 15:1-5. When you are done, go outside and literally bury this book. It can be in your yard or at a park. When you bury the book say a prayer thanking Jesus for this gift He has given us through His sacrifice. Don't forget to dig the book back out again.

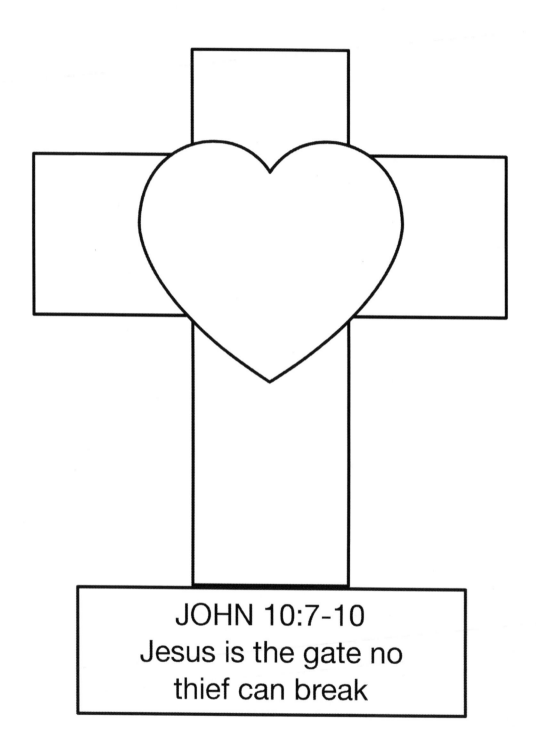

JOHN 10:7-10
Jesus is the gate no
thief can break

If a thief breaks into a home, they have one thing on their mind: "What can I steal for myself?" This is what the devil does to us. He is a thief who wants nothing more than to hurt you and steal what you have. The only way to fight back and win is with the strength of Jesus in your heart. Read John 10:7-10 to get a better picture of the thief and the Savior. When you're done, color the cross, rip it out of the book, and cut it into at least 10 pieces. Then tape it back together and back into the book.

Our aim should always be set to hit the mark of living as God calls us to. However, sometimes, we miss that mark. Does that make us imperfect? Well, sure it does. Does that mean there's no hope of forgiveness? That would be a solid NO! It is impossible to hit the target everytime, but the beauty of it all is that we serve a mighty God who still loves us. Read Romans 8:37-39 in your Bible. Then grab a drinking straw, a buddy, and start making a bunch of spit wads. Shoot them at the target on the next page. Everytime you or your partner hit the target, tell God how awesome He is. If either of you miss, thank Him for his grace of forgiveness.

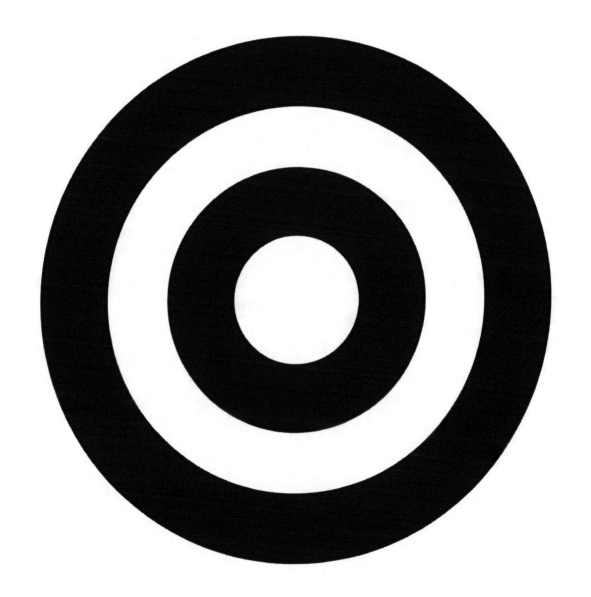

What does your heart reflect? In other words, when people see you, do you think they see an image of Christ's love coming out of you? We are commanded to take time to serve others. When we do, we begin to imitate the life of Jesus. He was known as a man who taught the importance of putting the needs of others first. If your mindset is more to serve, others will notice you as a person who loves to help. Read the following page in a mirror and then take 5 minutes to talk about why it is so important to live for others and not be focused on ourselves so much.

"As water reflects a man's face, so a man's heart reflects the man."

Proverbs 27:19 (NIV)

Everywhere we go, we should carry God with us. There are many ways to take Him with you. Memorizing powerful Bible verses is one way. Talking about Jesus with others and sharing your faith is another. Completing acts of love and grace to a stranger is also a way to ensure we are keeping Him close to our hearts and at the forefront of our lives. How ever you choose to keep Christ present in your life, work hard to make it happen.

Now tie one end of a string or rope to this book and the other end around your waist. Look up Mark 8:34-35 and read it out loud as you drag your devo book behind you. Read it out loud 5 times. You can run, crawl, walk, jump, spin around, or just mix it up as you read the passage.

As quick as you can, say 5 things that are super sticky. Would you say the way you live your life makes people want to stick to God? Love is one sure fire way to attract positive attention to Christ. When we love one another, you make it easier for others to want to hear about your life and faith in Jesus. It's this kind of living that makes a sticky kind of faith which keeps your friends wanting to hear more.

Read 1John 4:7-12 to better understand about living a sticky loving faith then cover this page with stickers. Use as many stickers as you can find. Try to cover every inch of space.

There are some things in life we might run to like a free all you can eat buffet at your favorite restaurant. Sin though, is what we should stay away from and resist. The temptation to do something God commands us not to do can be heavy and difficult to ignore. Using God as your strength, you absolutely CAN stay away and resist what is wrong. This is not always easy, but working hard not to get dragged through slime is better than belly flopping into mud right before you are supposed to eat dinner.

Take a moment and read James 4:7 in your Bible. Think about what this passage is telling you. After talking it over with your buddy, close this book and punch it away from you over and over again. You can even make funny noises while you do that. Each time you punch the book, tell God something you will do to stay away from sin.

DEAR GOD,

_____

_____

_____

_____

_____

_____

_____

_____

_____

_____

Love

_____

Do you know how much you are loved? Really truly loved? The amount of love God has for you is out of this world. He gave to us His only son Jesus so that if anyone - including you - receives Him as their personal Lord and Savior they can live for eternity in Heaven and not an eternity with the devil. God gave us Jesus because He wanted to. He knew we didn't stand a chance with out Him. The picture of Jesus, who was innocent, dying on the cross where it really should have been us, is the ultimate image of love. Remember how much you are loved. Read Romans 5:8 from your Bible and say a prayer of thanks to Jesus. Afterwards, use the blank letter to express how thankful you are for His great love for you.

Many people say they trust in God, but how much do you really fully trust in Him? An absolute trust in God means you daily lean on Him for help. Trying to live your life the way you think is best, instead of how God wants to direct you, is like ignoring all the street signs on the road and hoping you will safely get to your destination. Imagine how dangerous that would be. Not stopping at stop signs. Ignoring red lights. Turning down any street you think is the right one. But God won't steer you in the wrong direction. He even helps by providing warning signs of any dangers ahead. This means though, you have to fully lean on him. Not just when you want to or feel like it might be a good idea.

To help you remember this, read Proverbs 3:5-6 and talk about where you might not be 100% leaning on God. Then color in and cut out the heart below. Place it in your Bible on your favorite passage as a symbol to remind you how important it is to fully trust on God.

Proverbs
3:5-6

<u>WOW!</u>

Congratulations! You made it all the way through this book. Now for just one last devotional.

<u>Make sure to save this page for your very last entry.</u>

You have done so much to grow in Christ while having fun and wrecking havoc on this devo. Go back to the beginning and look at all you have read and learned going through God's Word. What was your favorite thing you did in this book? What is your favorite Scripture verse or Bible story you read (how many have you memorized)? Whatever you did to this book, know that now there is no other book like it anywhere in the world. It is now as unique as you are in Christ. It has a special flare that can't be found anywhere else. God's touch of love on your life is the same thing. You are as special and individual to Him as your book has become. Now close your book, and your eyes, and pray that God continues to strengthen you for this life. Trust me that I am also praying for you as well.

Scripture passages used in
Destroy This Devo

Bonus fun: Can you find what page in this devo each scripture can be found? Write the page number next to them. Also, go ahead and highlight all the Bible verses and stories you memorized. See how many you can store in your head and your heart.

_____Genesis 1
_____1 Kings 3:4-15
_____Ester 4:12-17
_____Ecclesiastes 4:4
_____Psalms 23:4
_____Psalms 100:1-5
_____Psalms 119:103
_____Psalms 119:9-16
_____Proverbs 3:5-6
_____Proverbs 10:9
_____Proverbs 27:19
_____Malachi 3:10
_____Matthew 6:25-34
_____Matthew 7:15-20
_____Matthew 14:28-29
_____Matthew 17:20

_____Matthew 18:15
_____Mark 8:34-35
_____John 1:1-5
_____John 10:9
_____John 10:10
_____John 13:1-17
_____Romans 5:8
_____Romans 6:22-23
_____Romans 8:37-39
_____Romans 10:9-10
_____1 Corinthians 10:31
_____1 Corinthians 15:1-5
_____1 Corinthians 15:9-11
_____2 Corinthians 5:7
_____Ephesians 4:32
_____Ephesians 5:15-17
_____Colossians 3:23
_____1 Timothy 6:12
_____James 4:7
_____1 John 4:7-12

About the Author

Andy is a Children's Pastor with 10+ years experience and was an elementary school teacher in both the public and private school systems for 8 years previously. For the past 7 years, he has been a full time minister at Treasure Coast Community Church (tc3.org) in Stuart, Florida. Andy earned his Bachelor's degree in Elementary Education and his Master's in Christian Leadership. He is a huge Star Wars geek, sports fan, and up for any fun outdoors activity (even the messy ones). Not only does Andy lead TC3 Kid's Ministry, but he's extremely active in the community including leading 3 on-campus Bible programs at 3 different public schools. He lives in Port Saint Lucie, Florida with his wife Amy and three daughters Elisia, Victoria, and Lilianna. They all love participating in children's ministry together. Andy believes children's ministry should be fun, engaging, and life changing with a side of wackiness. TC3 Kid's Ministry lives by the philosophy of connecting kids to the life changing power of Jesus Christ.

Printed in the United States
By Bookmasters